Softening Time

Also by Elena Brower

Art of Attention
Practice You
Being You

Softening Time

Collected Poems

ELENA BROWER

Andrews McMeel
PUBLISHING®

Foreword

Softening Time is a powerful work of art that asks us to slow down, land, and open. It is a gift to read this collection during a season of transformation, to immerse myself in the nourishing power of these words. Elena Brower is a true artist who uses the depth of her spiritual practice to serve humanity. Her poetry is some of my personal favorite, not only because of its beauty and wisdom, but because, when I read it, I can feel the power of her experience.

Elena and I have been close friends since 2017. She was one of the earliest supporters of my writing, and I am grateful I had the courage to reach out to her. Our friendship blossomed over the years. When we both lived in New York City, we would connect every few months and go on long walks in Central Park. I remember how I felt on the beautiful fall day when she first shared some of her writing with me, and I am so happy that even more people will get to benefit from her brilliance. She is someone I look up to; I take everything she says to me very seriously. Elena is truly one-of-a-kind—an incredible beam of light.

Softening Time is not only relatable, but it creates space for us to appreciate the small moments as well the life-changing ones. I hope reading Elena's poetry serves you as well as it has served me. May these words help you move intentionally through the world.

yung pueblo

For James and Jonah, for the continuous softening.

At every age since love was a possibility, there have been thoughts unspoken, mysteries revealed only in solitary silence, empty moments becoming holy within me. These are the times to practice softening.

This book is a journey of forgetting and remembering that.

Let your mind sit.

—Roshi Joan Halifax

Introduction

Outside my bedroom window, watching the neighbors negotiate their relationships while listening to my parents clumsily manage theirs, poetry becomes my most magnificent, healing secret. To express my emotional states through the written word is to dissect these states into digestible parts so I can guide myself through the misunderstandings of growing up.

This is still happening.

From the moment I learn to read, I devour everything I can: cereal boxes, books, poetry, magazines, novels. The written word provides me with ways to make sense of my experience, to let go of the unbearable pain that seems to linger in my limbs sometimes. Hours spent under my bed in the dark as a child, reading with my treasured flashlight, are a softening within myself.

Reading and writing teach me how to steep myself in the colors of both grief and joy until I'm saturated.

Our foundational challenge as humans in these times is to connect slowly, savor restful intervals, and find ways back to the words that give our daily activities deep meaning. What we need more than anything is profound attention to the instructive silences that dance between the words, to the glints of happiness that catch us off guard, to the depths of sadness that keep us connecting and listening.

The ancient human wish to make sense of things and understand the supreme mysteries is alive here in these words, collected and edited from poems and prose written since I was thirteen years old. You'll meet the influential forces in my life throughout these pages; from nature to my closest friends, from my teachers to my family, each has played some role in shaping and creating this time of softening in which I find myself.

May these pieces inspire your own Softening Time.

practice

sun rising in my bones
calling me home
       quiet refuge, body of
       learning and listening.
where unmitigated focus
seduces then silences me,
evolving patterns quietly.

I can see no other way

recovery

learning, landing.

heart grants boons
older than words.

      righteousness softens:
darkness to clear light again
hearing myself becoming
my dearest friend

      grandmother's heart
      prioritizes stillness.
      patience.

      simple medicine,
evolving broken legacies.

grand entrance empathy

morning

Punctuality means more to me as I get older, so I'm right on time. Setting down my things, listening to the remnants of last night's rain in the trees as the drops fall on the small stones beneath my feet, I tuck into an antique chair to wait.

The peeling finishes on the benches and tables mark the onset of rainy season here. Everything's just slightly off-kilter: this table is leaning a bit, that chair has an errant leg that needs to be nailed in. Something old within me finds this dilapidation charming.

The surrounding trees are the ultimate counterpoint. Ringing the perimeter of this place, these lush green beings offer evidence of what thrives when human fabrications disappear. Heavy with dew, shimmering in their morning magnificence, these ancient plants in their very existence whisper to us about our own experience. We can sense this connection in some canyon of our cognitive comprehension. Regal, regardless of size, innately moved to rise and reach with life. They turn toward the sun in any given instance, producing copious energy with every breath, giving me ideas about my deepest self.

Some words about believing in my own true nature arise and evaporate. For more flashes of understanding I sit very still and keep waiting.

considerations

silent, embodied words
the only reverence

subterranean

anguish pulses within my body.

circumambulating myself
       tending to the trees
       so I won't find myself
       in a heap of perpetual memories

no music, just cicadas,
       forbidding summer wind

       a universe of signals pointing

toward new topography:

kneeling-down surrendering,
animating the mysterious ending
       of this barely discernible beginning,

       time elapsing

every year around this time,
I think I hear the world collapsing

evolution

First, I'm food and water.
Stroller-pusher. Snack-maker.
Book-reader. Sleep-sender.

Each day I peel back one layer of protection.

Slowly I press you apart and away from me. I know it's time.

   I don't want to.

I leave the province of usefulness,
ensuring you touch into your capacities.
Sharing strength silently.

Together we locate
urgent compassion and
ask more questions.
   What's true now?
   Have we grown up yet?

Just ask the flowers;
they're always teaching.
Beliefs and constructs
blossoming and
releasing

one thought at a time

floor of my first studio apartment
beneath my forehead, kneeling,
  at home here.
  altered, high.
two decades later
a world away
upright in my favorite chair
at home here, fine.

almost eight years
since I changed my mind
became myself

gift of age, gift of quiet, gift of time

  today discomfort reigns
  am I a good mother
  decent friend
  loving partner
would they be fine if I
  disappeared

stranded with staccato, threading questions
momentarily wishing for that high again

take me ruin me
forget me remember me
release me remove me
help me save me
remind me erase me
inhale
emptiness
exhale
emptiness

on the inside

there,
stepping out of violence

I choose myself today
this continuum
listening energy

expanding resilience
home frequency

when I close my eyes:
today's shade of sunrise

pigtails

when I was four, I told you that you looked
too much like the babysitter
>   right away you cut off your pigtails and replaced them
>   with stylish feathers

in my dream tonight I'll apologize to you for that
and a few other things

>   like turning my face when you try to kiss me
>   pulling away when you reach for a hug
>   inexplicably ashamed of your love

tiny rejections that mean nothing to me
(I'll readily forget them, until you're gone)
to you they mean more and more
(once you make yourself at home in my refusal)

but.
when I apologize tonight, we'll go backward in time
to your gleaming brown eyes
listening for the sunshine
your right hand clutching mine

dreamland forgiveness
the most unforgettable true kind

sometimes and suddenly
standing at the sink
your presence lands,
wraps around
safe
and sound

patience

Evening finds me near the piano, dishes done, sitting on the spare
    chair.

Occupying myself with orders for kitchen supplies and a book on
    Audible,
later than my son said it would be. He walks in eventually,
taps my shoulder knowingly.
Feels more like an old friend to me than he did yesterday.

We don't speak. He kind of winks,
takes his seat and begins,
his whole body emitting Beethoven's Moonlight Sonata
like he was born with this music within him.

He delivers it with the patience of a much older man.
The way his hands get lighter during certain phrases
takes my breath away. Suddenly and without warning,
my mother is present within me. I can smell her.

Understandably she wants to be with him, right now, up close;
I'm the best vehicle and she knows it.

He finishes most of the piece, his promise complete, eagerly heading
back to the virtual space where he's seen for different reasons.
Another prowess deemed impressive by his peers.

When he catches my tears, coming nearer, he's standing over me,
his hand on my head drawing my cheek against his belly, quietly.

Yet another door into the temple.

remembrance

mind softening
dwelling in trust
      returning to presence

almost every gesture reflects this
      humble remembrance

A B C

I'm twenty-three when I walk by this place, staring at textiles and expensive, aspirational balm for my fraying New York haste. I want to live there. Most days I go in, saving bits of money for some silken sky-colored pillow I've been coveting. Someday I'm going to create something that will be shared here; no idea what just yet.

I'm thirty-nine when I begin co-creating a book on which I've asked two friends to collaborate: photographer and stylist. After one day together, they partner up to create, bonding over the pursuit of magic; months after their first meeting one of them vandalizes the steps of that store with those words.

In Pursuit of Magic.

Store owner asks me if I know whose words those are. I do.

Together they begin creating, elevating, reminding of the real pursuit. Remember seeing those words on walls, sidewalks, benches? Apertures.

I'm forty-four when this place becomes our Saturday morning church: a place for our listening, our momentum toward grace. Souls lining up amid meticulous displays; tiny vases full of faraway flowers; books, fabrics, and beads sourced from places of prayer. Awed and moved by the tiny temporary altars, something changes in these days: something softens in the way we'll live in every corner of our homes, for the rest of our lives.

We arrange our mats respectfully; we sit. Somewhat nervously I organize notebooks, flowers, inviting breathing, heart, softness. We reset our neurology, situating our bodies into shapes that change our brains indelibly; certain songs, scents, glimpses of art have a way of bringing it all back to me.

It takes about ninety minutes. By the time it's over, we've released all haste, more light and slowness in our now-kinder faces. We remember that we'd forgotten again.

Our practice, our medicine.

anything will help

Slanting late-day sun barely allows me to make her out on the median.

Her cardboard sign says in neat block letters that Anything Will Help.

So carefully written.

My brain turns to the lock on my door, but my right foot moves first. I brake. I open my window. I'm shaking.

I reach for the emergency bill my mom always told me to keep in my wallet. Folded, crisp. I extend my arm out the window with it. Neither of us expects this. We lock eyes.

"My mama told me to keep emergency bills on me."

She's obviously here, energy in the car. I sense her hands patting my head like when I was extra sad during the worst of the uncertainty, waiting for me to feel something softer.

"Thank you so much . . ." The woman's eyes hold me; her words trail off.

Recognition, ancient and quiet, descends; neither of us can move. She adds, "Stay safe," which is when we realize our four eyes are all filled with tears, silently staring a second too long, just the right amount of time to feel the one single heart beating there on that median.

She stands tall and proud; I'm in my car with my mom's ghost patting my head so I won't disappear, tears falling onto my lap,

Long line of cars waiting behind me, patiently.

asking

fourteen years, one month, twenty-five days.

here's that feeling I'd read about,
the one I swore I'd avoid.

tools dissolving in tones and interruptions,
love fracturing in words.
timely individuation.

no resources I can name, no glory.

welcome to the province of helplessness.
unfamiliar territory.

chances

This moment, a hinge
This word, that habit
This thought, that glance
That shape, this dance
Our capacity to measure up
stitch together
take chances

Where consciousness flows
in degrees and grades
Where love knows no bounds or lanes
Where my light and your light never fade

held

I'm nineteen; we meet during a tender time.
She's single-handedly shifting an assumed, toxic paradigm
that tells me I'm never going to be a writer.

Beautiful because of her giant mind,
she's not much older, but she *knows*.
Words inhabit her with a fierce, mysterious majesty.
Words are at home in her wise, confident body.

She presides over a long table in that historical building,
first floor. Smallest class I've ever known;
I'm afraid to get it wrong yet somehow owning that
I'm not alone anymore.

I begin listening. I fill myself with every phrase,
decoding some of the treasures.
Heart still swells upon reading them,
decades later.

"Let the poem work on you," she tells us.
"Let your heart be held by every word."

Ithaca, 1988

open letter

the confluence of forces
leading to this door opening:
simple to decode.

earnest teachers
eager students:
humans being.

      artful projections
      simultaneously accurate and
      doggedly imprecise.
      both sides.

do we choose to take aim and accuse
or do we choose the quiet lens of compassion
in both directions?

      we acknowledge our blame
      and all roles in our pain.
      we accept ourselves.
      we accept our humanity.

      we carry baskets of forgiveness.

      we remember that someday,
      nobody will recall any of this.

nothing

tip of a leaf absorbing midday sunlight
this one waves at me,
tiny gem of aspen,
sounds of my mind forgetting
all the differences, targets,
grievances

nothing left but light
and drinking it

the edge

only empathy can usher you
from the prison of your past
that childhood
those imprints.

turn your attention
squarely inward
replenish your reserves

grant yourself the quality of
energy you give so freely.

if this makes sense,
           your beginning is unfurling

this conflict is natural

Allow yourself to evolve.

>You are a creature of
>distinct beauty,

daily discovering what it means
to be human
to be close to yourself
to stake a claim on your own happiness.

To relax is not to collapse, but simply to undo tension.
Tension is a theft.
Be in adherence with the present moment.

—Vanda Scaravelli, *Awakening the Spine*

older

I sit down this morning
and you're here with me;
inside my mind,
some ancient need to fix things
is bubbling into my morning writing;

your words sound as real as my slippers sitting next to me.

> *There is nothing more important than the truth.*

I sit very still so I can hear more of you.
I make giant spaces around my heart for
this fresh field of understanding.

> *They are hurting, so they hurt you.*
> *Remember this. It isn't personal. Nothing is.*

Looking toward the closest pile of books,
all my doubts silence themselves.
You remind me again.

> *This is when nobody needs fixing.*
> *This is when eyes close softly and listen.*

your release today

Quiet times bring thoughts
coming
        going. Investigating.

        Mind empties as swiftly as it fills.

Encountering great doubt,
I allow time to pass us by,
this doubt and me,
until a dignified demeanor speaks.

I am of the nature to grow old.
There is no way to escape growing old.
I am of the nature to have ill health.
There is no way to escape ill health.
I am of the nature to die.
There is no way to escape death.
All that is dear to me and everyone I love
are of the nature to change.
There is no way to escape
being separated from them.
My actions are my only true belongings.
I cannot escape the consequences of my actions.
My actions are the ground upon which I stand.

—The Buddha's Five Remembrances
Presented by Thich Nhat Hanh

the mothers

This morning,
the trees teach me how to stand,
to let the nourishment rise up from inside,
to breathe with each other,
to listen for each other,
to keep communicating,
to share the deeper healings,
to rest when it's time,
to pace myself.

The greatest teachers in our lives are often found in our families.

—Sherri Mitchell, *Sacred Instructions*

empty house

Sitting still I can hear primordial ache
resolving through my being

wind in this
empty house

If I sit still long enough
the air shifts,
hearing far beyond myself
into an easier silence now.

Intimacy redefined.
I write this down in celebration of our wordless quiet.

moon and snow

snow and moon are now
the same colorless color
original mind

gateless

It happens quietly.

Grandmother's heart
inhabits you
with tenderness
with equanimity.
Equal presence
victory or catastrophe.

Gateless gate,
eternity.

one body practice

gassho, deep bows:
I forget my own name.
hauling wood, shoveling paths,
sweeping mind, clearing plates.

today, again, patterns on parade,
various old messes I've created.
I release them to the field of practice.

gassho, deep bows:
turning the light inward.
finding my way out.

belle

What ties us together all those years
remains a mystery.
I'm not the eldest or the prettiest
but here we are, unconditionally knowing.
I rub your feet with the knowledge that I'm
learning how to care for the first time.

You're falling asleep on your couch
smiling; what you've always needed
is right here: the follies of the upstairs neighbors.
The Price Is Right.

My first taste of deep listening, of
collaboration. Closeness.

Fifteen years later I'm hiding
on Gouverneur Beach while
you're dying
but I'm too nervous to go and see;
for the first time in my life I'm
convinced I cannot.
Frozen to this island,
frozen smile at dinner,
frozen heart in my chest,
grief relentlessly knocking.

I hear you say my name in my sleep
the night you die.
I've never told anyone that.

Sometimes I play it out in my mind
going further than what *was*

to what is truer.

Images well up like little confessions:
I hold your feet like I did for
            your daughter on her last day
I whisper in your ear the endless love like I did for
            your daughter on her last day
I wrap you in the stunning and believable
            light of your own soul like I did for
            your daughter on her last day

our house

late at night you sit near me,
making space at the dining room table,
moving books, the piles of
nourishment for my writing;

you're slightly sideways and hungry

while the English muffins toast,
          I count blessings
while you tell this week's stories,
          appreciation shining through your
quiet brown eyes,
your tiny bitten nails
evidence of

your heart's catastrophes.

your consistent reverence
is an unseen force
holding you together.

the way you see the best in people
makes me weep most days

Whatever we frequently think about or ponder upon, becomes the inclination of our mind.

—The Buddha

questions of sustenance

Why are you here
What are you nourishing

Can I trust you

Are you growing your soul

Is there direction to your questioning

Are you listening

Are you moving and strengthening your body
to affirm its power
against the specters of the mind
Do you know there is still plenty of time

Are you willing to disagree harmoniously

      Are you able to see this heavy emptiness as a door
      Are you ready to die

her hand

It was her hand out the driver's side car window that started it all.

I don't know if I'd describe it as a fall. It was her hand that I finally saw in my mind's eye under hypnosis for smoking cessation. She was already sick, but I'd already welcomed her perfect imperfections into my heart.

My mother cared so thoroughly. But she would trade her happiness for mediocrity, hoping for an impossibility to sustain her identity.

At a certain point I had to tell her I hadn't come to parent her; therefore I was unable to hear her:
my own imperfect, twentysomething
boundaries.

In our communications now, however, she understands me perfectly.

dear thirty-one-year-old self

Shower yourself with empathy every time it hurts.

No need to give your power away or prove your intelligence.

Love your mother more; record your grandmother's voice.

Respect your body, your lungs, your light.
You are surrounded by benevolent forces
        and you never need to be right.

Treat yourself with deepening, widening kindness.

maps

I don't need strategies anymore

I'll just sit here
empty out
again

making these glistening, harrowing moments
into maps for the future,
lessons for different teachers.

forgive your parents
my favorite feature

dear seven-year-old self

dark, sad, tiny thing
i see you burying yourself under the bed
behind the navy flowered dust ruffle

your glasses keep getting caught on your way in

you're crying under there
with your art projects piling up
and
the stuffed animals who still talk

making magic with the colors
behind your closed eyes

what i really mean to say
is that i love you

and
one day, you will be lifted up
one day, you will find love, deep love and
you will have a son
and he will see you with a clear heart

you will become a swirling concentration
of gifts and blessings

just wait

almost

She's staring at me, her little-girl eyes barely in her head, heeding my instructions to just stay put. She's barely here. Moments earlier she'd collapsed in my arms as I'd helped her walk from her bed to the washroom; now she's miraculously managing to stay upright while I hold her shoulder with one hand and dial this ancient touch-tone wall phone with the other. I've never been more on purpose, more afraid, or more present in all my life.

Maybe it's three or four seconds that pass. Our two souls stare into one another and wonder if this is where it all ends, a lifetime of giving and receiving, doubting and believing, right here in this bathroom. It's luminous between us.

Door swings open, nurse barges in and presses me aside, taking my mother in her capable arms to get her back to her bed in order to measure things—her heart rate, her pulse. My mother is only a few days out of a stem cell transplant, at ground zero, as weak as she will ever be in all her life. I'm certain that this day marks the end of our road together—our roles had reversed so dramatically just then that it seems the only proper next thing.

She proves me wrong.

From that moment on, and for the five years to follow, every second some sort of healing will happen—in her cells, tissues, bones, in our patterns. I couldn't have known that I'd have five more years with her—we make every visit count, with only one big blowout that I can recall. The last glance we share as she leaves my apartment, she's a little girl again, impish eyes waving goodbye after I'd massaged her painful left side with a balm I'd made, the last time.

I feel then something I'll never forget. I sense what will come next.

Five days later, sitting in her home office, she'll fall to the floor, all those chemo drugs rendering her heart muscle half dead, only to be resuscitated by my father for her final twenty-four hours of semiconsciousness. She'll spend her last day hearing us remind her of her love, her beauty, her wisdom, our thankfulness.

That moment in the hospital those years before makes her real last day one of the holiest days in my life, holier than childbirth, full of prayer and meaning, connection and clearing. Death no longer to be feared here in my heart; it's the most sacred commencement.

a love story

When this time of year arrives, I'm back
in the car, no more than nine or ten, outside school.
She has curly hair, vibrancy,
a cigarette, held casually, elegantly.

She loves me.

She says it incessantly and
even when I say I want her to stop saying it,
her love puts me at peace.
So familiar, that feeling;
she always knows what I need.

I now see.

All of that love just seems normal to me.
I imagine all the moms do this with their babies.
Now I see that they don't.

When this time of year arrives, I'm back
in my son's bedroom, he's nine or ten, we're playing air hockey
on his bed; the phone rings.
She's had a heart attack; she will likely not last.

And now we're packing—books, games, comfortable clothes?
Funeral dress? "Remember to bring nice shoes,"
whispers her voice in my head.

Not familiar with this feeling, I'm wheeling
the clothes, the shoes, her grandchild through
Penn Station. Everyone must sense it from my face.

> The last time. The last time I get to kiss her
> or resist her
> rub her feet or hug her,
> the last chance to return all that love to her.

I will never forget that next day,
my cheek resting on her belly when it rises for the last time,
listening for answers I already have.

mountains

Learning to make monuments to emptiness

my quiet mind
words on a page
feeling myself dissolve
dancing alone with the sound of bird wings.

"Look up," you smile.

I'm so small.
Tiny pants, shoes.

"That cloud! Can you see it?"

What I know now of true love carries your imprint.
Your voice is right here.

Nothing but spaciousness
Atmosphere

holy

compassion reminds me
eyes, neck, hands show me
years passing

separate enough to be received

becoming holy
now even the trees speak more slowly

Slowly we
make our appreciative response.
Slowly appreciation swells to
astonishment. And we enter the dialogue
of our lives that is beyond all under-
standing or conclusion.
—Mary Oliver, from "Six Recognitions of
the Lord"

holes

back then we had streets, bicycles
wooden clubhouses, lemonade stands
we shouted and ran for the ice-cream truck
and happily hid in anyone's bushes for
neighborhood hide-and-seek

nobody was dangerous then

years later I run away and hide in the tall portico of
my first school, sitting there for hours,
snacks, books, journal,
making sense of this unspeakable sadness,
first taste of knowing that family
doesn't mean forever
even though it does

decades later when I'm lied to,
I'll stay very still so I can feel the
lacy, tenuous threads of my heart
unspooling precariously throughout my body,

shooting stars creating human-sized
holes in my unwavering belief

lenses: one

Less visible
Less afraid
Stare at it long enough
And what you're seeing changes

lenses: two

You'll get where you were going
But you'll never know what
You might've missed

lenses: three

What questions did I forget to ask
New outlines
Dimensions
Light dims
More softening

lenses: four

Am I merging with earth or sky?
Is there ground beneath vaulted vision?
Do I want to escape this
   Dissolution

Or walk toward it?

lenses: five

Nothing disappears in the dark, does it?

lenses: six

Said, unsaid
Evidence of radiance

> Giving is a great prayer

lenses: seven

We said we'd find one another
Define one another
Free one another
Countless times

library

We walk in together, holding hands, until we don't. In front of us, the lady at the desk seems overly enthusiastic. To our right are all the children's stacks, books with letters too big and pictures too obvious. I've spent hours there, but I'm older now.

We turn left instead.

The metal shelves loom large, the ones for real people. Stairs and desks and books with no drawings whatsoever invite me to come nearer, promising their mysteriously rich abundance of information, escape hatches, treasures beyond my wildest dreams. My mom knows exactly what it all means, and where she's going, until she doesn't. Just before she heads toward the fiction buffet, I tip my chin up in the direction of the desk I'm choosing, to which she smiles her impossibly welcoming brown-eyed gleam that still comes to me in dreams. She strides away confidently.

We trust each other here. This is our place together, where we can safely, triumphantly separate. We claim our shared independence here, the only place where we can do that, until years later when we find ourselves sharing a cigarette on a porch at a spa in the sunshine, our second and final trip together. The joy of smoking neatly lingering alongside the knowing that her days are numbered and I'll one day soon be motherless. But I digress.

Sitting down at my chosen library desk to do homework feels like I've cracked the code on adulthood. She's all mine for a time, even though she's over *there*. Books are everywhere, worlds into which I can enter freely, neatly. I've got papers to write, but everything I need is nearby. It's here that I learn to synthesize, to cope with mountains of detailed information by selecting, prioritizing.

Hiding in my work like all the other adults do.

tribute to practice

First.
To those mornings:
the ones that feel most like
the home of the lie
the war in my heart
every thought a loaded gun
   this body the enemy

   hurting halting hating
   when it's so painful

Then.
To this day:
the lie dissolves again
art appears
   new dimensions
   heart pacing:

cadence of freedom
dreaming by deed

Practice:
        holding no tension
        expanding again

finally arriving at an agreement with myself

what if your practice is an art form
not a path, but an expression

2 a m

His growing hand touches my head, so big I don't recognize it.
Pulled out of one dream into another.

He silently beckons me to follow him down the hall,
full of purpose. Now taller than me, leading wordlessly.

     It's been months since this last happened.

Silently he points to my old side of the bed,
motioning to me. Sleep *there*.

     A foot, then a hand, finds mine.
     He even lets me hold the back of his head like when he
was tiny.

Breathing deepens, sleep descends, time stops again;
     I'm staring.
     Heart beating beneath his broadening chest,
     same face, same heart, same love, same nest of silence.

New quiet for both of us.

what I don't know

The way your eyes close halfway,
full-wattage smile when you look at me,
tells me it was all real.

Even when I questioned your love.
Even when you were too distracted,
when you couldn't find any peace.
Even when you lied.

I know you're sorry now.
But

        I still don't know who I am sometimes
        because of all that.

Then there's the way you lean in to hear now
(all those years of music *this loud*)
to be certain you don't miss a single syllable.

The way you grab my hand when I talk to
make up for lost time.

The way you open car doors.
The way you didn't before.
That particular elegance arrived more recently.

The way you let my boy hassle and tousle you,
the grin that emerges even when he gets rough with you:
I feel your tender release into elderhood
but I don't know if
I even want the whole truth. Thank you.

Older, wiser, more present, less afraid.
I wonder if my eyes will close the same way.

sitting

Sun rising, heart presence
mercifully strips away certainties

I sit to stay alert to the mystery

Sometimes my own presence is
the one I really needed

My deepest satisfaction now is entering into the inheritance of my own life. A realm over which time has no sway.

—Anne Truitt, *Yield*

tenderness

i'm six, seated on the sink cabinet,
door closed.
No glasses on.
My little left crossed eye struggles
to stay centered;
i'm opening myself to an inexhaustible ask:
who are you?

WHO.

      Are you?

Speaking to the mirror
contact with something bigger;
the question works on me silently.

      There are no answers here
      but knowing arrives
      i'll let myself be held by this
      high tide of quiet
      for the next little while

sister

When I first realize I can help you, it's too late. They're in charge and they keep me away. They don't know any better.

They aren't taught that the truth actually can be a precursor to freedom, so they persist in keeping us apart, opting not to involve me in the vital work of taking care of you. This perplexing abstraction of distance remains the most vexing circumstance of my young life.

You're the prettiest doll I never get to touch. In the other room, just there, down the hall, five steps away. You even look like me. I'm equal parts smitten, forbidden, heartbroken beyond recognition.

I don't find the words until a whole life later.

Helpless in my homemade barrettes, knowing what I don't know yet, feeling the presence of your separateness, trying on a sense of sorely unnatural independence. I easily focus through the accrual of time to hear the fraught, clipped tones our parents use when they try to make sense of this furtive cacophony: Your suffering. Theirs.

Their abject confusion slices through dozens of years, inhabits our cells when we try to make sense of the trials you endure during this tenuous, unspeakably painful early life of yours. Once you learn more, we're able to piece this story together.

My helplessness leads to a lifetime of longing to be of some utility to total strangers. Yours matures into a tender, fiercely loving, loyal woman who knows precisely who she is and what she represents, with utter certainty. You raise a stunning man in clear possession of the richest textures of loyalty, capacity, confidence, intelligence. He'll never actually know how much his life has meant to you, will he?

What remains are these patched-together words to express the poignancy of my conviction:
I only wish I could've helped in some way, back then.

And a lifetime of diligent study shows me a possible alternate reality:

Pigtail rubber bands with strands of your hair there, next to your head. I lay my hands on your small, fragile body and sing you slowly to sleep. Your pristine, perfect face settles into tonight's version of peace. I quietly and silently walk myself home to my room. You, comfortable and easeful: everything. The pale pink carpeting. The steam heater that hisses my system to rest. The snores and finally contented sighs of our parents.

I easily wend my way from one reality to the other, tears streaming, daydreaming it all into my body. Healing happens. I make sure you have plenty of signs.

small moment

Morning finds me on my favorite chair,
cushion slightly damp from last night's downpour,
sun tickling the tops of the junipers and piñons.

Day opens up to welcome me.
In light of the unceasing flow of change,
this feels like some kind of preparation.
Sitting is really just noticing,
helps me have mercy on myself.
How utterly human of me to
grasp and perseverate,
mind going this way and that.
How normal of me to forget
that I'm my own oldest friend.
Noticing helps tenderize things.
Sitting consistently transforms what we notice.
The practice of observing and quieting the mind
helps us see that passing feelings and thoughts
don't need to disturb us
unalterably.
And we don't need to keep chasing after them.
Noticing thoughts come, then go.
Tranquil heart.

One moment.

spring

Walking with green trees
the light changes my mind

devotion help me

summer

Light gives all presence
choosing a lazy, softer
lemonade evening

fall

When trees change color
I become a falling leaf
please can you catch me

winter

Light slants, wind speaking
secrets smiling in midair
nobody knows me

ancestral intervals

The circle that Suzuki Roshi draws silently
in the air with his hand
on his deathbed, in response
to his dear acolyte, who asks

> "Will I see you again, after you've died?"
> The circle.

The dark, soft pink hug of the morning,
birds still tucked away at the edges of the forest.

The silent, declarative embrace when my son
presses his face into my eye socket
so strongly, my distracted angel:
> I'm steadying myself to absorb every moment of contact,
> profound appreciation filling me, like during fresh rain.

Wind whistling through the piñons,
leaf songs from another world.

Last breath of my mama,
my cheek on her belly, skies opening.

Gentle crunching sound of cones
and branches underfoot,
scarlet late-day majesty.

My man catching my eye
in the kitchen,
words of dinner
as inexplicable gratitude rises up in the
center of both of us like water in a tree.

End of the meal,
quiet of the night descending,
sliding door opening,
smelling the forest breathing.

rare moments

"You must become friends with the silence,"
she teaches.

How, then, right here at this dinner table,
shivering chaos, am I five years old
in my striped shirt and culottes?

Aren't I grown up yet?

No silence to befriend
just humble piles of pain
sitting uncomfortably
eating quickly

One of us silently speaking
to dead people,
attempting to hide the fact that she's
begun to cry, but no more taking sides:
small victory.

This happens
about twice a year.

Then empathy emerges
running rings around my heart.

Becoming friends with the silence.

mother of all things

To the Mother of all things
May I feel fully the fullness that is you
that is me
that is all

May my brokenness be broken open
May I trust that this existence is Love
May the faces that are not my own fade away

May I digest and absorb the healing
medicine of my own inner world

I am not healed

I still wonder if I could've been of more use, more presence, more comfort, more grace.

I recall messages of "Come visit" and that look of "When will I see you again" on her face. Out of the corner of my mind's eye, I see her there, resplendent, brown hair, faded bell-bottomed jeans, leaning toward a tiny version of me.

In such glimpses we two are alone with the trees, the green grass, the bluest sky, and the flowers. This is when she is my entire world, when I can recall details of her skin, seams on her shirt, her smile a soft landing for my doubts. About everything.

Her devout commitment to being a good parent and wife

coexisting with her need to become herself,
to live the fullness of her own life.

I feel both every time she holds me.

Forty years later I feel her looking through my own eyes most days, sifting through the words I *could* say, love cascading vaguely through my chemistry.

It's been seven years. I am not healed.
We both go on in here,
soft landings
never-endings

never

never have I felt more my own
ever increasingly more at home in here
experiencing this slower cadence
that reminds me to wait

soften my space

you've left me with a shorter story of
sunlight and patience

a movement toward poetry

which is where it always needed to go;
I just couldn't have known it until now.

I love you I miss you I
wish I could call you
so
quietly I find myself checking in with you,
this new pace of truth

what if every gesture expresses your
present glimpse of enlightenment

Love isn't something you feel, it's something you do.

—IN-Q

faith

the strongest force is not gravity

it's curiosity
a holy map to that which
you are healing
within yourself

every incidence has its own intelligence

> you can change the world,
> but only through this
> burgeoning
> unfamiliar
> intimacy with yourself
>
> what if you're just here to develop
> faith in yourself

fragile gifts

trustful surrender
and self-study
gateways to
inherent beauty

in the name of creation i question this
obstructing numbness

in the name of destruction i question this
blessing in front of me

terrifying collision of energies

i slow myself to a standstill
to remember
these fragile gifts
these living,
breathing mysteries

imperatives

Place yourself in the way of grace:
sit still, let the muse
find you and fill you
so creativity can emerge.

Get good at what you do.

Forgiveness, again.

Be even more adaptable.

Lead yourself and others with tenderness and ferocity, equally.

Efficiently use what you have.

Rest often.

Take this precious glimpse of stability into higher and wider
contexts;
and when it works, don't doubt.

Then thank a difficult person for showing you your priorities.

Lean on the Universe with your honesty.
Ask for signs.
Receive them gratefully.

Disentangle from the evidence
so you can see the unseen.

Look at the places where you feel you aren't being heard,
and see where you're not listening.

you are all women

In your husband's car
on city streets
laughing till our bellies ache
intimate sweetness
two young women discovering
unexpected, unconditional friendship

In ceremonies of love
afternoons of listening
evenings cooking elaborate meals
gorgeous tableaus coast to coast
music for every moment
shared truths only we will ever know

In the moment you give birth
to yourself; when you hold
       your daughter's porcelain lifeless body in your arms,
      you are awake, receiving, your heart carrying
this profound medicine forward

      You are all women

You are all women when that
part of you comes alive
birthing the two of you

You are all women when you
tend to your mother's cancer
stumbling and loving your way through
her pain, her departure

You are all women when the
brave choice to sit at that ancient typewriter
and write it all down becomes the only one you can make

You are all women when you
listen to yourself in new ways and
your reality unswervingly changes

I am

I am that four-year-old with a patch over her eye, scorned and ridiculed.
I am that five-year-old who has trouble using the bathroom in kindergarten.
I am that six-year-old who doesn't read quickly enough for her teacher.
I am that seven-year-old who doesn't have many friends.
I am that eight-year-old who longs to be cool.
I am that nine-year-old who gets in trouble for talking in class.
I am that fifteen-year-old who blatantly lies, disrespecting her teachers and parents.
I am that sixteen-year-old who's stoned in class, sleeping on desks.
I am that seventeen-year-old who tries to control her life by eating almost nothing.
I am that twenty-year-old who sacrifices her health for her grades.
I am that twenty-five-year-old who gives her body away to be loved.
I am that thirty-five-year-old who is scared to have a child.
I am that forty-three-year-old who still feels lost.
I am that forty-four-year-old who's just begun her sober journey.
I am that fifty-year-old who's beginning to know who she is.
I am that fifty-one-year-old, writing it down, shedding her skin.

I am that prayer.
I am the one who prays. I am the one who answers.

twins

Obviously we belong to one another
from some other stratosphere;
your face and mine seem
likenesses from another time;

I see you and know you instantly.

You impress me with your mind,
your willingness to learn,
your mothering, partnering
and
damn woman
you're just so good at what you do.

What changes me most, though,
is our banter.
The pointless conversations
that travel on forever, weaving our way from
gardens to apocalypses to family and back again,
deepening validation from another dimension.

mate

can't remember
any life without you near
even though you're so far.

brother:
I have snapshots.
Sydney, Brooklyn, Gerlach.
Guiones, Santa Fe, Thredbo, Taupo.

you, supine, mistaking one drug for another,

receiving the vital recalibration

you, in your zone, face behind the camera,
cajoling me to move and shine
this way and that
yes, yes, and yes
lights held high
           bugs swarming
           body drinking sunset.

a collection of
captures we'll never, ever forget
your friendship,
lifelong medicine

the lamp we've lit

Sitting across from you that day
over and over in my mind replaying it,
seeing his face the moment I see yours,
knowing and not knowing.

You come closer and breathe light into the most
unalterable connection of my life,
this daily unfolding of empathy,
knowing and not knowing.

We learn to live separately and together, still.
We turn corners together, still.
We hold each other, raising him together, still.
We find languages of support and lucidity, still.

Cooperative clarity grows,
bodies organize into knowing,
conscious infusions of care in shared dialogues,
spoken and unspoken.

This big, bright lamp we've lit
keeps elevating our tender, earnest dynamic.

Knowing. Not knowing.

. . . the protective instinct that attracts you to what encourages you.

—Rebecca Solnit, *The Faraway Nearby*

kitchen prayer

balmy, tender memories
smitten, ruined, you and me

our quiet, redemptive symphony
becomes a distant buoyancy

those nights i wished i could
lick the future from your skin

but today i'm wiping down the counter
so silently
again, leaving the balled-up paper towel
      to sit there
      act of defiance

walking extra slowly so as not to
      jostle this heart in my chest
afraid if i move too fast i might forget

      the way you loved me when i wasn't
      prepared to love myself

*On the edge of awakening this morning,
I slid into the happy consciousness that
my life here is just right.*

—Anne Truitt, *Daybook*

trails through trees

cloudy November morning, exhausted, Bowery and Houston.
in comes your handsome, well-dressed, salt-and-pepper energy,
all seawater and depth, eyes, giving,
yes.

your kind presence filters in.
my mother will love your
blue-eyed wonderment.

next chapter is handed down
when your hand lands on my chest.
words are happening. but not quite yet.
we wait for life to grant us our opening.

i'll never forget your big paw on my heart.
the feeling of wanting to start something.

by the time we see one another again,
you're striding toward me; i'm so far in.
i invite you to bring some of your things.
i bend and fold and mold myself to your kindness.

sobriety, deaths.
illnesses, madness.
creativity, impermanence.

somehow we maintain a distance,
a nourishing mystery, still softening.

moments string together; life glistens across quotidian landmarks.
the brushing of teeth, unknotting of tiny chains on bathroom
sinks,
sunshine on silent balconies.

fed, flourishing, private, seen.
now holding hands awkwardly on narrow trails through trees.

[Poetry] goes where words cannot go.

—Joy Harjo

your silence

I can claim years of learning from the silent prayers you carry.
Becoming a different person each time I look into your eyes.

Deepening art is made together:
your body, my words,
my body, your needle and thread,
your kind eyes and barely perceptible voice
speaking wordless volumes
to my eager, appreciative heart.

Silent sittings, amid your friends, your art.
Nature walks, prayer tents, music.
Colors of every leaf and tree,
crocheted snacks,
cacophony of galleries,
mysterious underlying ease.

Many years of this.

That day, that frantic call to Kings County Hospital,
your pleading eyes that made mine weep instantly.
I'll never stop thanking the cop who saved your life.
How we all had to recover with you.
How do such things happen to such a tender human?
I'm still asking.

On the other side
a quiet ferocity to meet your gentleness
a stunning womanchild to absorb your willingness
a sterling creativity that knows no rules, no needs, no bounds.
A vast, humbled community receiving and mirroring
your childlike, expansive unity.

The privilege of elderhood:
still cooking and creating.
Somehow we made it.

angels do exist and trees are so special

the rest

something about you draws me near
from moment one.

on some grassy field,
we're introduced even though i feel like
i know you already and am smitten.
your height, your elegance, your
patient eyes. your words. your drawings.

moments arrive that we'd never have planned.
realizations that we'd both been
mistaken, in our own ways.
bonds are created.

fortified by deepening wisdom and
some unspoken understanding,
we don't need sentences to be
sure we'll remain safe landings
for one another.

we meet at intervals.
we build in alignment.
we craft quieter futures,
savoring our
synchronous assignments.
build. rest.
listen. rest.
learn. rest.

landlord

At a pivotal moment, a mutual acquaintance sends you.
Serious at first, then the wit seeps in.
This will clearly become a deep, lasting friendship.

The day you finally bring me home, there she is,
dining room table, homeopathy books strewn about,
smile beaming across the room to me:
She's fearless.
She's family.
And because of her, you're one step closer to me.

One day not too long after, you become my landlord
and that loft becomes my history,
my marriage,
my kid,
my whole destiny.

Those lights on dimmers change it all.
The steam shower, the giant tub,
the way you both help me locate my clarity
right there on that fire escape.
So many hours of laughter I trace back to you.

That chapter ends, which is when
the new love you find makes you whole again,
moves me to settle into my own understanding
of partnership as salvation. Thank you for that.

I still read your daily emails.

I love that we get to grow old on the same shoreline.
Your presence in my life means more than these
flimsy words
can ever express.

softening time

Sky full of clouds, pensive piano notes in my ears, about fifteen minutes from home with all the groceries. You call me with gravity in your voice, which is rare. I pull over instantly.

Yes, cancer. Yes, surgery, yes, chemo, yes, radiation. Yes. My best friend.

Yes, healing. We're holding one another from two thousand miles away, hugging over FaceTime, struggling to find the words. When I finally find mine, I tell you I'll shave my head when you do. Together we've lived in the same house, studied, played, traveled, had our hearts broken, gotten married, had babies. You're clearly ready to take on the true healing, though, and that's what this conversation reveals.

The softening.

Strangely, your softening becomes my own; I can still see how I allow agitation to seep into my day, hurling me quietly into anxious reactivity. Over months, I watch from a distance as you become more vulnerable, less afraid. I feel you shift and am moved to ease up on myself, to drive more slowly, to listen for the holiness in the voices of those closest to me. It's still happening.

When we finally shave our heads, I worry the new look might change me, harden my heart somehow; instead I find myself with more time and space to think and feel, to rest and be, as though I can take myself less seriously. Somehow more intentionality is accessible without all that hair, that whole personality. And I can hear the forest outside differently.

Witnessing the most fearsome possibility has raised us up, brought us closer to ourselves and to our own trust. This surprising, stunning chapter is still open for both of us.

completeness

ride up to me, haze of dust
perfectly managed dose of drugs
slowing mind down just enough to

      glimpse your inherent poetry

the way your dusty rose
falls just over your shoulders,
i know your heart instantly

      with reverence; together, free

something ancient here within us,
old truths to keep witnessing
nothing i cannot say about this

      completeness

I'm nobody! Who are you?

—Emily Dickinson

asking for a friend

when we meet on that roof,
you make me laugh within
seconds.

you offer me a level of warmth
that couldn't possibly align
with the otherworldly beauty of your face,
your outfit. i barely accept it.

i'm sure i'll never be cool enough for your
friendship, but you insist, and we find it.
your mind is what keeps me deliciously twisted.

how on earth you could know *that* much.

we laugh with, and at, our men.
we disrupt outdoor yoga classes.
we consistently dream of hot dogs.
we're still learning how to listen.

growing older with you
and your mind
and your man and your child near
is one of my wiser moves.

of this i am certain

wait, what

bandanna on your head,
you march right up to me after class
and tell me we need to be friends.

i have no reason to disagree with this.

but if i were to document the scenes that ensue,
the fluency of this evolution
would barely be believable.

from seedy fire escapes to
perilous construction zones
to perfectly lit dinner parties,
strings of tiny lights
placed at just the right height.
all of us beautiful, ready.
ripe.

from the tippy tops of ballrooms
watching your man steer
thousands of shirtless revelers
with the flick of his finger
to the tops of mountains,
blinding blizzards teaching us how to see
to your delivery room, there he is,
the most perfect, free being.

from the silliest borough-traversing drives
to every exalted dream realized,
the beauty you create brings big, fresh
tears to my eyes

thirty-one

the bar in soho where it happens is long gone now.

i turn thirty-one, you walk in,
toting my favorite rubrum lilies
and a smile that lights up the room
making me forget whoever else is there.

i have no clue who else was there now.

you hug me, you take my hand,
you sit down next to me and remind me
of what it means to have a true friend

and the beginning and the ending are written.
all the milestones are covered,
the finest men become our lovers,
the children find their way to us.

your skills of connecting and creating
producing and relating
become legendary.

also your family.

but it's that smile, that birthday, your
confidence in knowing i needed you that way,

that's what did me in. i'm forever your person.

ELENA BROWER

nameless

tall glass of water
elegance from other lifetimes

       traces of which
       inform your walk,
       the way you hold your gun
       the eyes you have for your dog
       how you care about this dimension
       and the others

your silence gives me vital clues
about how to merge with myself

the way in

at first i was afraid of you;
i forget how or where we met.
enamored of you and your freedom,
i was so full of gravity then.

and you were better at being different.

but you saw me somehow; you let me in
my nervousness became architecture for
something holy, which becomes our primary circuitry.

two little girls.
thank you.
that's what friends do.
our alliance still helps me see through things.

and when we find ourselves pulsing apart,
the currents of creation, the layers of art, hold us in.
rose petals on chipped sinks.
heart swells. parenting.
text threads, rich histories.
costumes, bars, memories.
poetries, prayers. certain uncertainties.

you keep opening
the immutable, ineffable part of me.

elder sister

At a handful of inflection points across my life, your hands appear in front of me,
traveling, serving.

Your deepening reverence sparks mine.

A canopy of respect hovers over us: taste of tea, taste of time.
The leaves speak volumes in your silence.

Careful piles of bowls and humble wooden utensils are a sumptuous extravagance.
Meticulously laid textiles carry the barely perceptible blots of past ceremonies.

And each small, aging blossom placed across my purview transmits a detailed story of relationship and resurrection.

Every movement of your fingers is a bow from a distant generation.

You are flawlessly precise, patient. I feel your studentship first.

In time, your humble, ancient mastery stealthily emerges.

and you

how you suffered so dearly
for what I experience as such sanity now

your elegance, your sadness, your luminosity

I can sense both the cost
and, in the end, the fact that there was
no loss, actually:

gateless gate, eternity.

between us, the way is none other than one awakened mind
darting between and around us, so many little paintbrush motions

reminding us to stop thinking and remember this ocean
            of silence

perhaps

every day
the truth happens

perhaps today's fresh acceptance is
all the aptitude we need

one more silence

your kindness is food for me
your example becomes
a perfect reason to
stop ruining my body

today your eyes and encouragement
help me welcome this process of
growing older elegantly

but it's when you wish me
happy birthday this year.
after all those hours of work together,
yours becomes the first and only
message of silence

which floors me
and shakes me,
reminds me of
a whole new place
where narratives
just drop away

floating, forest-bound

the reverent way in which
you fold the dirty dish towel
and place it as though
you're handling one of our children

your willingness to bring me in
closer to your heart
your unstoppable kitchen skills
your burgeoning wisdom

i've watched you over years as you've
become yourself,
walked through a fire that burned your insides
played hide-and-seek with the universe
until you were found, treasured

which is when you slowly remembered yourself

remembered that you can stop
barreling downward
and look up

floating, forest-bound
loving, warm eyes listening to trees and sky

your grace

elegance, gliding into my class
i'm bowled over by your kind eyes
there and then i decide that

      i deserve you.

the friendship deepens, trust emerges
the way you treat me changes me

      in your words i learn my worth
      and in the way you revere my work
      and in the softness you lend even when
      it's so hard to understand anything

you transcend time and space
especially while dancing on
cocktail tables,
which is where your shining smile
teaches me that it's okay to
whisper into Stevie Wonder's ears
what he already knows

second floor

The giving and receiving are slow, but they happen.
A life of partnership ripens on that second floor
where I do a good deal of growing up

Window opens,
I hear my name
your kitchen becomes
my favorite haven

You offer your friends, your trust,
your dog on my lap
your heart's tenacity
your ferocious knowing
your relentless listening,
which you don't give lightly

You offer counsel, refuge
love, unconditional
art, irrevocable

I walk myself there
as a new person each day
ready to give and receive
with you

I can still smell it: whiffs of

burned burgers, roasted nuts
incense, weed
dosas and humanity
Soho was never the same
when you went west

gramercy

I think we were in the Flatiron first,
somewhere where the lights were that perfect pink
and of course you were dancing

I was riveted, smitten with both of you,
the way you moved like you'd known one another
for lifetimes, which of course you had:
when I met you and your brother that night
I knew it was for life

The times we sat on your floor,
smoking,
wishing for love and clarity through the
hazy veil of our latest escape hatch

The times we walked the dog,
questioning,
praying for the right guy or the perfect time through the
heavy heat, summer nights of New York City

The time we gathered our toddlers in Rome,
swimming, triumphant,
realizing we'd chased and found our dreams,
and there they were, pushing matchbox cars in diapers,
pristine window of awe and motherhood

I will never stop missing your energy
your laughter
your family

In the most unexpected moments you're still right here with me

l o n d o n t o w n

Your accent nailed me initially. And the fact that you wanted to be
my friend.
After that it was your hospitality, laced with curiosity
and your deep acceptance of me, granted generously.

But that one night when I thought I'd lost you, when I held your
limp body so close to me as though willing you to
come back
        to life:

it took so many minutes and cigarettes for you
to remember what you'd never forget.

We follow one another through doubt to softening,
from preaching to listening,
reminding one another that the holiness is
        in the giving:

I hope you finally feel
who you've become on this planet
and that your journey matters

altars

i meet you in that holy place
        you bring me home to
        help you change
but you end up changing me

it takes years to see how deeply

your homes, full of majesty,
teachers, imagery, pottery,
meticulously placed pockets of history
softest materials and dignity

        being near it all alters me

you carry me across the world
expose me to beauty and depths of
reality and prosperity i'd not otherwise have seen

you bring me closer to my own reckoning
        i'll never forget how you let me in
        i'll never stop thanking you for
        that sacred beginning

then suddenly

In my dream,
        you're in a full mustard-yellow cotton prairie skirt
        cowboy boots
        perfect hat
        you're maybe thirty-five, smiling, vibrant

then suddenly
some mean face arrives;
you're turning in another direction,
which takes my breath away.

then suddenly
you're smelling my neck
for the first few minutes arriving on that
mountaintop, friends for life,
mybeautifulwife.

you gave birth twice, you lived, you tried
we were miles apart for a long time
then for one phone call you almost came closer,

which only moved you
farther away in the end.

hard to admit it,
but this ache remains

Is the poem doing what you want it to do?

—Joy Harjo

your softness

across a table of holy water and sacred sound
you come to trust me

i am starstruck but capable
>>> i give you my all and my best;
>>> admiration deepens, refreshes itself

the softness with which you move about the world
transforms my understanding of myself
and your long limbs,
your graceful fingers i'll never forget

>>> your dignity harmonized by your silliness
>>> your impeccable features overpowered by kindness
>>> your expansive mind overshadowed
>>> only by your generosity

because of you
>>> i keep searching for all of this within me

seekers

you reach out your hand;
your sari touches me first, i think.
the room is crowded but we manage
not to blink when we connect.

the true world of silence is about to
descend upon me;
this world will lead to a new translucency
in about twenty years.

but the seriousness we share throughout that time
is punctuated by big belly laughs
the moments of loss outshined
by a deep reverence that lasts
despite all the distractions
and disappointments
we'll support one another steadfastly through
all of it;

the empty, holy places where
nothing and everything happens
remain so close and present,
same as in that temple,

all those seekers needing a seat

doctor

I would not label ours an auspicious beginning,
but we make up for it here,
at the end.

our in-between time,
so close and yet so far.
both doubting and wondering
holding the door slightly ajar
with small offerings and silences.

light dances through that tiny opening,
just waiting for one of us to catch on,
which we eventually do.

now when I look at you,
all I see is your heart in there
your insane intelligence that keeps
unfurling in front of my eyes
studying, listening, absorbing,
witnessing, teaching, becoming.

the honor of iterating in this
lost-and-found sisterhood
is immense:

without you I'd have no idea
that being in a body could feel
this good

people who have experienced deep suffering
and are still gentle with others
do not get enough credit
to not let the hard things
that happened to you win is heroic work,
to drop the bitterness
and still live with an open heart
despite it all
is a massive gift to the world

—yung pueblo, *Lighter*

c e

your fragility:
I want to help and hold
and care for you from the first moment,
      so I stay close

your style:
I want to learn and grow old with you even during
these long distances,
      so I stay close

your commitment:
I want to remind you how crucial you are
as I watch you try to heal,
      so I'm still here

up fourmile

when we first meet, you have an earring in your nose:
i judge you

you hug me like we've known one another for lifetimes:
i decide to love you

you sit next to me, a brother, for decades
you hold my hand, remind me to dance,

you soften life's blows in ways that make me grow closer
to myself

you tell me things that i like to think
you don't tell anyone else

you welcome my men, my kid
my questions, my messes
you send me music to fill up my senses
you make me grow wiser by
showing me how to drop all my defenses
and laugh
again.

forever thank you

let go

It starts on my studio floor when you take too much of something;
I forget what.
So I lay you down in front of my little altar there
and tell you,

> Rest here. You are protected here.

Hours, years pass. I think I leave to teach a class,
come back and find you still there.

> I smoke several cigarettes.

You emerge hours later,
thankful, closer to me now.

And in the end,
all I did was show you how
> to let go.
> And then let go again.

Filed under: how our friendship commences

hey girl hey

I think you fell down in my class that day.
Pretty sure it was my fault; either way we started out laughing

Cut to the roof of that house,
properly soused, getting thrown out;
was I trying to tell Rihanna
how much her work means
to all women

as if she might not know

Luckily you follow me down,
teammate.

There are long walks, pride parties.
Partners coming, going.
Weddings. Solidity.
Adulting. Victories.
Deepening uncertainties.

How surprisingly much you've come to mean to me.

every seed knows what to do
the challenge is convincing it to wake up

—Chris Ferreiras

gifts

presence this moment
growing older is a gift
forgiveness reminds me

my happiness
is a teaching
in itself

quietly

To this scaffolding of appreciation
  I bring my whole brokenness

To fortify this sacred catastrophe
  I weave these threads of contradiction

To wake up to active hope
  I let the world hear me

To reflect the artistry of my respect
  I arrange my seat quietly

  remembering again the fleeting nature of this life

delicate mists

I am free to choose the environment of my mind

      to stay open when
      some part of me wants to close

      to release the energy
      that isn't my own

      those delicate mists
      of pain and trembling

again

A prayer rising is what we've become now.
We ask for kinship. Simplicity.
And I thought I'd been listening
but here comes a
finer sympathy

the medicine of letting go

again

the only gift

Together
Listening
Something changes

Lulled into this fresh field of quiet understanding
Carefully providing for each other a softer landing

Seeking the subtleties of love
within the appearance of the difficult

       skimming toward infinity,
       acknowledging the vibrancy,
       the peace we didn't know we had.

You are the right sound, the light in me,
the taste i savor, the silence i covet

Your trust is my temple

Watch me wind myself around you
tangled toes till we're gone
       ribbon for the only gift

turning the light around

This silence intoxicates me
I slink around my own house as if in a dream
The whole earth a realm of source, seeing

I'm turning this light around
restoring myself with what I knew when I was

hiding under the bed in my
tiny pajamas, hearing things:

       everything will be all right
       sometimes people forget

surrender

Surrender
            is not a loss

it is the giving up of
hesitation
excuses
and fear

            that have no place in your life any longer

our friendship is based on what isn't happening

The words we share
always ringing through time
like the clearest bell,
reminding.
The approval we seek, forever granted.

We reach out when we need it.

Steady and present, every ask feels like

some kind of magnetism drawing us closer
across distances. The trust, though,
is the real bond.
To trust you,
to know that you trust me with your
words, your walls, your poetry,
this is the most generous boundary.

a part of things

First, your words make their way
from your pages to my mind,
admiration swirling between us,
elevating our early exchanges
in ways I'd never dreamed for myself
in this lifetime. I mean that.

It doesn't take long for us to find it.

When that dire time falls on you,
a pile of heavy stones,
the medical facts and realities
bringing you to your knees, some days.
Walking up and down Madison together
helps lighten the weight for some moments.

Still I see you shining, writing it down.
You find new voices and ways and choices.
You give me books, phrases,
generous thoughts that
lift us both. You point me in the direction
of writers who will help me walk through
what it means to grow older.

You even frame the art I send you.
Which makes me feel
so much a part of things,
the very definition of endearment.

The need is not to be a poet or be heard. The need is to listen.

—Zenju Earthlyn Manuel, *The Deepest Peace*

currently

dropping this composition of forgetfulness
       witnessing myself into being

inviting silence as the primary container for
       my grief

extinguishing the need to perform

acknowledging the unknown
as the most welcomed antidote

exposing myself to voices of vulnerability

       resting my exhausted certainties

It's like that planet we went to. The one where all the separate creatures share a single memory.

—Richard Powers, *Bewilderment*

ELENA BROWER

the lawn

A few laps is all it takes.
I remember many of our words
and even our shared steps.
Nervously but assuredly
opening our hearts
before we really know or trust,
talking together while our lives
are under construction,
making clear impressions
that will continue, uninterrupted.

Just the walking together is somehow
enough. Your faith in my experience
becomes a beacon; my few thoughts
about self-care slip into
your consciousness.

We remind one another to keep learning,
to keep changing, to keep letting go.
Not that either of us really needs it, but still.
We manage to help one another.

Our common bond is held in your own words:

the greatest gift
sadness gave me
was the motivation
to transform

—yung pueblo, *Inward*

This body we thought so important,
it's a porch, that's all.
I know this, but I don't know
what to do about it.

—Naomi Shihab Nye, from "The House
in the Heart"

what if

what if your practice is an art form
       not a path, but an expression

what if your work is to arrange yourself so that your seat
       reflects the simple artistry of your respect

what if every gesture expresses your
       present glimpse of enlightenment

what if you're here to develop faith in yourself
       to forget yourself
       in order to remember

keep letting go

keep letting go

even your awakening
even your realization

Acknowledgments

I began writing this book as a child, scrawling longings in treasured journals with tiny locks on them. Thank you to my editor, Melissa Rhodes Zahorsky, for your gracious, graceful clarity and wisdom.

Thank you to James Benard and Kevin Sullivan at Benard Creative for your artful, thoughtful mastery on the cover.

With deep gratitude to Roshi Joan Halifax, the teachers and staff at Upaya Zen Center, and Diego Perez for pointing the way inward.

This collection is for all the hearts who've walked with me, some of whom are honored in these pages.

Roshi Joan Halifax
Wendy Johnson, Sensei
Monshin Nannette Overley, Sensei
Natalie Goldberg
Wendy Dainin Lau
Kozan Matthew Palevsky, Sensei
Kodo Noah Roen, Sensei
Jonah Lyon
Judi Brower
Isabelle Drath
Ric Furry
Arnold Brower

Jessica Brower

Libby June Weintraub

Carrie-Anne Moss

Pete Longworth

Dr. Anthony Lyon

Pedro

James Benard

Susan Cianciolo

Tracee Stanley

Michael Tucci

Christy Nones McKenzie

Ally Bogard

Jordan Daly

Athena Calderone

Tali Magal

Chloe Crespi

Dana Bauer

Baelyn Elspeth

Sierra Campbell

D.J. Pierce

Alicia Boyes

Zofia Moreno

Lysa Cooper

Alysa Weinstein Gravina

Nadia Narain

Lori Goldstein

Kate Thorson

Christy Turlington Burns

Nikki Costello

Dr. Gabrielle Lyon

Cristina Ehrlich

Joshua Onysko

Mads Kornerup

Gray Hudkins

Laura McKowen

Dani Shapiro

Diego Perez

Works Referenced

Page 26
Vanda Scaravelli, *Awakening the Spine* (New York, New York: HarperOne, 1991), 53.

Page 29
Thich Nhat Hanh, *The Heart of the Buddha's Teaching* (Berkeley, California: Parallax Press, 1998), 115 - 116.

Page 31
Sherri Mitchell, *Sacred Instructions* (Berkeley, California: North Atlantic Books, 2018), 147.

Page 51
Mary Oliver, *Devotions* (New York, New York: Penguin Publishing Group, 2020), 126 - 127.

Page 68
Anne Truitt, *Yield: The Journal of An Artist* (New Haven, Connecticut: Yale University Press, 2022), 15.

Page 96
Rebecca Solnit, *The Faraway Nearby* (London, England: Penguin Books, 2014), 26.

Page 98
Anne Truitt, *Daybook: The Journal of An Artist* (New York, New York: Scribner, 2013), 23.

Page 134
Yung Pueblo, *Lighter* (New York, New York: Harmony Books, 2022), ii.

Page 150
Zenju Earthlyn Manuel, *The Deepest Peace, Contemplations From A Season of Stillness* (Berkeley, California: Parallax Press, 2020), 85.

Page 152
Richard Powers, *Bewilderment* (New York, New York: W. W. Norton & Company, 2021), 158.

Page 155
Naomi Shihab Nye, *Words Under the Words* (Portland, Oregon: The Eighth Mountain Press, 1995), 101.

Andrews McMeel Publishing
a division of Andrews McMeel Universal
1130 Walnut Street, Kansas City, Missouri 64106

www.andrewsmcmeel.com

23 24 25 26 27 MCN 10 9 8 7 6 5 4 3 2 1

ISBN: 978-1-5248-8263-1

Library of Congress Control Number: 2023931222

Editor: Melissa Rhodes Zahorsky
Art Director/Designer: Tiffany Meairs
Production Editor: Meg Utz
Production Manager: Julie Skalla

ATTENTION: SCHOOLS AND BUSINESSES
Andrews McMeel books are available at quantity discounts with bulk purchase for educational, business, or sales promotional use. For information, please e-mail the Andrews McMeel Publishing Special Sales Department: sales@amuniversal.com.